COLORING BOOK
FOR TEENS

Simple Designs for Beginners

1.

the Stars are calling me I have to GO

www.ingramcontent.com/pod-product-compliance
Lightning Source LLC
Chambersburg PA
CBHW081604280526
45788CB00011B/3543
* 9 7 8 1 5 4 6 7 9 1 4 5 4 *